MADELEINE GAGNON

STONE DREAM

TRANSLATED BY ANDREA MOORHEAD

GUERNICA

TORONTO – BUFFALO – CHICAGO – LANCASTER (U.K.)

2010

Antonio D'Alfonso, editor
Guernica Editions Inc.
P.O. Box 117, Station P, Toronto (ON), Canada M5S 2S6
2250 Military Road, Tonawanda, N.Y. 14150-6000 U.S.A.

Distributors:
University of Toronto Press Distribution,
5201 Dufferin Street, Toronto (ON), Canada M3H 5T8
Gazelle Book Services, White Cross Mills, High Town,
Lancaster LA1 4XS U.K.

First edition.
Printed in Canada.

Legal Deposit – Third Quarter
Library of Congress Catalog Card Number: 2010925318
Library and Archives Canada Cataloguing in Publication
Gagnon, Madeleine
[Rêve de pierre. English]
Stone dream / Madeleine Gagnon ; translated by Andrea Moorhead.
– Translation of: Rêve de pierre.
(Essential poets series ; 172)
ISBN 978-1-55071-318-3
I. Moorhead, Andrea, 1947- II. Title. III. Title: Rêve de pierre.
English. IV. Series: Essential poets series ; 172
PS8576.A46R4813 2010   C841'.54   C2010-904514-9

STONE DREAM

ESSENTIAL POETS SERIES 172

Canada Council   Conseil des Arts
for the Arts   du Canada

ONTARIO ARTS COUNCIL
CONSEIL DES ARTS DE L'ONTARIO

Guernica Editions Inc. acknowledges the support of
the Canada Council for the Arts
and the Ontario Arts Council.

CONTENTS

I

DAYDREAMS 7

II

THE PHOTOGRAPHIC EYE 59

III

PROMENADES 85

IV

READING THE STONES 111

No power will crush under its heel this happiness
of being here and being no where, of vibrating in
unison with a universe that once again comes out
of its sordidness undefiled.

Jacques Brault
Au fond du jardin

I

DAYDREAMS

There
when centuries and centuries
snow
across
stone

There
when the sun touching
the eye blinks

And when eternity
seems behind
suddenly remote
abruptly
particles

Sands

A noise
that displaced nothing
sound entered
time as if earth

Or this mark
of migrants
when they die on the way

Impromptu

Or perhaps
a man's hand
before conglomerate

Or a woman's
before night

Sediments in bodies
before
sundials

Everything is possible
everything

Flesh perhaps
deposited there

Or even cities
dropped from space

The countryside would be
this compressed memory
of ancient metropolises

We don't know
those silent people
and gold-bearing veins
heads hidden in their hands

Their books
then

Therefore
cities
men women
rushing along

Perhaps children
gone prematurely

When the uproars
the earthquakes

Or even wolves
sculpted there
heraldic pelicans
caught in their jaws

If
following the thread
memories of primrose
or lupine

If
under the eroded quartz
transverse hordes
defying boundaries

Sword blows on the rock
fragments of wars

But nothing speaks any longer
when blood
has dried

Pebbles thrown
before prehistory

Mothers' bellies
birthing slits
and the faces

Promises
after history

fruits and wine still flowing
mouths
juices

Doubtless houses
sited on the escarpments

Crevices
first measures
(wailing)
People forged their destinies there

Music

It's time
says sand

The drop of water
rings in turn
(insinuates digs)
salty

Silence

Forgotten cities
suddenly
their backs bent
turned to the wind

It was necessary
to scrutinize stone

Starry mirror

Then fossils
fish leaves
it's immortality
after decay

Things represent
what no longer is

The living blind
pass by

Come back salt
mouths
No no
don't leave again

Mute note
on the horizon

Life intermezzo

From the cliff
slip
soot lost thirsts
sudden modulations
the source

Often in winter
ice sheets

Shout under ice picks
frozen utterances

Memory of night
thaws

That snaps in a dream
roused
right through the skin
blank walls

Stretch marks of battered
lands
spring always
returning

Reed or stiletto
bird feather
bear tooth
or eagle talon

It's all
headed for the alphabet
one day

The same
or another

The scent of strawberries
changes listening
and deciphering

The scent of stars
in flower

Noon midnight
the earth rolls
towards its setting

She kisses the water
skipping stones

Lips caressed even amorously

And even lips sealed
entombed

The sky is a bowl
of ink
People dip in

Letters or figures or notes
stream
People paint and count

Measured out
in staves, tables
in notebooks

The moon wore
a party hat
mirrored in the ocean
inverted rock

From one schist chamber
to the next
and from balcony to door
the moon keeps watch

Crowds stamp their feet
wedged together dead-tired

Cities' slumber
there and here
after the death of cities

Sleep and dream
the murmured word
the cry

The megalopolis feigns
forgetfulness

A heron passes
supersonic

Cliff of dreams
Babylon slumbering
ethnic
tower

Then the sirens
medusas in the dawn
wind

Scream or groan
nothing is clear

The ear dull
drowsy
mollusc

Everyone does it
our steps add
to the impressions

Our steps our hands
our feet our eyes
on the distant horizon

Then back again

Dying is slow slow
Not wanting to die
their death

Hanging on
by their nails
sheer walls
the earth a fjord
blood

Time no longer presses

On this rampart the death rattle
earth hugged
tightly

Other scratches

Stiletto-sharp
Breath flayed
its ink

From all sides come
compelling
reminders

For example in the morning
in the creek
this placenta stuck
to the sheer rock

Seaweed giving birth
to stars

Formerly peaks
these mineral mothers
collapsed

Not far however
a field of strawberries
lips juices

It's time
everything gleams

If
pursuing the thread the salt
the mother
in the leafy rocks
the rain

If
the other day
wings
fallen
into the moss

And cascades

Choruses

The hand gropes

Ten fingers chiseled
into the buried
face
alone recount
the ancient shipwreck

The fingers the cheek
sunken drops
furrows

Fossils:
leaves petals
human secretions

Languages of women's
bellies

And the guns
the swords
tongues shrieked

Librettos of cliffs
and far off
partitions
of hordes of sons
murdered

At noon
this blaze

Residue of hunting fires
buried customs
for them
even the words
are forgotten

Hunting fires
sandy firewood
but also the birds
flying in formation
into the bright light

One sees
these residues
in the form of journeys
vividly depicted

One muses over
(and attempts to decipher)
this geometry
of birds

The walk continues

At the bottom of a grotto
stuck to the wall
totem from another era
displayed – old palm
not far from a mouth
open to cry

She would have said
(that seems audible)
on her death bed
in her childhood tongue:

"Bring me two rocks
to look at."

The lips and the hand
know
that she did not ask
for two stones to contemplate

No
these are two rocks caressed
before the last breath

But the voice
childhood's voice
on the final evening
imprinted

The voice the hand
the crumbled rock

Last desire expended on sandstone

Elsewhere deep in the deserts
particles of sandy residues
symphonic echoes reverberating
(almost mute)
the voice the hand the supplication

Exist in all languages
confiding in the earth
each with its childhood words

Muffled in the morning
the noise has wings
white on white

But the song of the ice packs
muffled

Snow is deaf in February

Nesting no one knows where
the eye is blind to the horizon
all the birds are holed up
underground

Sedentary from the cold

Yesterday today
we understand them
(so little)
only in summer

Slowly
the band lifts
flat table set up
that stretches and stretches
into the dawn sun

Hoarfrost

Feast promised to the birds
remaining there

Glasses set on marble
watery dance floor

Humans' ecstasy

The banquet continues
There is enough
for all the famished
wanderers

Plates lichen
rocks and minerals
beaks open
cups clink

Crystals and clinking
signaux pour les voyants
this was written by a human

Friends, come
glass in hand

"Is there a life
before death?"
he had asked

Go by, earth dwellers,
and come back
thus sings very softly
the profane
prayer

Anything goes

So raise your glasses
bons vivants
nursed on the moment

Sucking gulping up to the end

Quick another drink
just to imagine
the eternity
of the one departed

Another sip of time
amusingly endowed
with ubiquity

In full swing
at its zenith
a voice which says
don't want to leave there
don't want to go away

It says: "Don't give up either
you who are there
I don't want you to go away
still desire the interweaving
of our lives."

On the icy rock
shaped like an armchair
facing the sea
I'll wait for you

Tears frozen
until spring
will melt
like the rest

At your return

But when you leave
if before me
you do go

Don't look back

If

in such states
the end is sensed
no fences
however

One advances despite everything
step by step
peeling off the ghosts

Even far away drawing
final alphabets
traced
in rust

Believing they're eternal

While the birds
peck away at
crumbs
we take our leave
of the feast

Each in our own way

No two
alike

Someone will hear
at the evening hour
a music made
from absence
from noise

Someone else will be this hearing
brought back
to zero

And someone else again
blind
will never stop
stretching out his hands
as far as possible
from the body

To locate other bodies
in space
and touch the universe

With the return of ice
their common shroud
no passerby will know
even the most discerning

What transpires
under the magma

No one passing by
no dreamer

There
when centuries and centuries
transect her

Aggregate

And loom's capture

II

THE PHOTOGRAPHIC EYE

Shattering aerolite cracked this rock into a thousand pieces, billions of years ago.

I kneel and knead. I learn about matter with my hands.

How many birds, fish, or mammals have left feathers, scales and claws here? We don't know.

Is there any memory of the impact's impression?

At my question, however, something stirs in the inner-ground.

There were cyclones and anticyclones. Here.
That's evident to the naked eye.

Or to the photographer's gaze. It's a question of
framing. The geometrical form subdues the
apparent jumble.

After, watch the shadows, seize the light which
flattens itself and escapes. Click. The old torments
of matter die down.

Become what will be watched, immobile. Such is
the destiny of minerals.

The photograph espouses their mission.

"Éternel et muet."

It's a dream of stone.

It concerns mortals.

No humans at the time of the great glacial thaws
that left this. This museum came from them.

No eye to see the upheavals when that occurred.

No photographs at the time of the great
catastrophes of stone. And that's what I see.

Not a single painting either.

Writings, even less so.

The music of crackings and upheavals fell silent.

Wagner and Mahler imagined snatches of it. Their fury accompanies modern tragedies.

Today's music captures these sonorous dreams of memory's flight.

Nothing to register the effect of gigantic blocks of ice, the splitting of masses, their dissolution, the deluges which ensued.

Nothing for the bursting of planets, the meteor showers, the birth or the extinction of stars.

Nothing to preserve the images.

Except what recorded itself, here and there, with each revolution of the earth.

May I contemplate. There.

Contemplate and study. Matter teaches as much as people. Sometimes more. That depends on the states.

First there is the dream. It encompasses study and contemplation. One tackles it without speaking.

Photography has no sound. It's mute and does without words.

Words are there before or come after.

Slow dream and the body in motion. At the beginning. For light and shadows.

But also for angles, positionings.

And the photographer's eye roving, seizing what will not be in the image. Chosen at this precise moment. Precise and long, sometimes.

Like a poem or a tune. Or a painting.

Motivated by things seen, but which come from within.

First the dream.

The study leading to the act of the image-poem happens during. That particular dream.

Then suddenly, nothing left.

The simple adaptation to what will be.

Suddenly the shutter's click.

And already the promise of what will be seen.

Some day.

Already the memory of what was, then.

Already the memory of what has been.

The game of anticipated recollections.

In a split second, the future perfect winks at the present.

The thought of the moment when the eye had apprehended this subject.

The thought, then.

After photography, it was written in the sky that people would invent cinema.

Between the two, the necessary electricity.

In the poet's heart, gaze locked on this tight space, the painters' accompaniment.

The love of paintings.

Living witnesses, faithful hangers-on.

Millennia embraced.

Something stirs in the inner-underground.

Between the eye and the hand that isolates with a deft gesture, something knows.

Doesn't speak.

Single wing skirting the living walls. Opaque.

Right up to the line, opening through which one perceives the printed trace.

Slit of light (greetings, bygone sun and moon and all the stars that brighten the darkness!)

Through which musical fantasies still slip.

A score presented to anyone wanting to play it.

Before the notes, the stave aligns its silences.

Instances when one pauses, listens to what unfolds, resonates.

Over enormous mute rocks and scattered stones, capricious mountain horizon.

One would say that the irregular mass is going to sing, lungs swelled, orchestra of cellos.

To the ear, the Partitas of Bach.

Single notes, then all the baritone trombones, cloak and caress them warming even the summit of the highest cliffs.

After the image – the pose – music alone returns to the universe the questions it wrote, committed to tablets.

Music, tongue of extinct gods.

Universal.

During this celebration of hearing, the vacillating heart confronts vegetation (trees, branches, leaves, and flowers) that has become petrified, stone.

How to render texture, make time's passage felt? The strata, the sediments, the ages?

Lying in wait with its questions, the heart, the soul's eye.

How, for example, to show this petrified tree trunk, immense Doric column collapsed in the wilderness?

And the petal of a little-known flower engraved underneath, in the very middle, like a hieratic alphabet?

Close the coffer of enigmas, forget the tools.

Wait for the song.

Patience. There's the lesson, the ultimate, age-old proposal, despite urgency of this instant.

We aren't even close to a paradox.

We're taking this one whole, a little like a very young woman closing her arms around the child who came from her, no longer hers.

Nubile, filled with this hope, still uncertain, she would walk with this treasure clinging tightly to her belly, to her breast.

Calmly, she would stride over obstacles, doubts.

She would see, beyond the horizon.

Because there was, just a moment ago, the entire sphere, illuminated.

She could swear it on the flesh of her flesh, rocked by the rhythm of her walking.

Out of the depths of the shadows, there is death, immutable witness.

And this life, advancing double life, entirely given to the rising sun.

Don't make any more noise.

Put down the camera.

Something is happening, this morning, which does not concern you.

Or maybe, slowly, descend the promontory. Greet the proud young girl passing by, silently bearing her destiny.

One would think she's praying. And that she's offering you her hand.

One leaves the passing girl, but she also goes off with a firm and supple step, for some unknown destination; it really doesn't matter.

In any case, what pulls her away seems good and joyful.

She displays a young mother's simple gravity, like a responsible pilot who doesn't lose north.

She has the sextant riveted to her gaze.

One leaves the passing girl and, checking gear, sets off again climbing.

Why?

Because this sun, at this precise moment, illuminates an enormous rock in the water.

Because one never saw it like that before.

Because the colours have just invented its form and time is racing over it.

Thus, men, women, cities, now grasp it.

And children, no doubt, marine monsters chasing them.

Because of this coppery orange, autumnal red on the sandstone, woven into the sky's reds, the water's.

Three different reds that black and white cannot illustrate.

Incendiary monochrome on the liquid divan.

Just evoking it, brief figurative poem that consents to the inferno.

Also caressed, white and black letters on the river-leaf, on the ocean-chapter, on the edges sheltering the shipwrecks.

One after the other. Continuously.

And the images cross the letters, phantoms of lost reality.

Just to revive the blaze.

Might as well forget technical incompetency.

Flagrant, even for someone who knows nothing of it.

Thinking about what isn't known to render what is seen would be to abandon everything.

The walk and the expedition.

And this reporting of images which one cannot renounce.

It's quite true that without them the story book would have escaped us.

With it, history itself would have been swallowed.

As for the aftermath, one already makes it into a mountain of miracles. Until it crumbles.

One already imagines a thousand other ways.

Of seeing and living.

Stone, rocks and boulders, pebbles and lumps of coal, sand and wind.

Colours and their shades and the people who wander about inside.

Each and every one, filing by with their own reflections.

We exist in time which carves and imprints. We steal a little eternity from it.

Suddenly the course is suspended, the proof will be there, one clutches its promise to one's chest.

On paper there will be the faint suggestion of resurrection, until it too crumbles to dust, some far-off day when we no longer exist.

Until scattered it adheres to the vast agglomerate.

III

PROMENADES

Go off somewhere, not very far from the little
house overlooking the open ocean.

Go off and remember, with each walk,
monuments visited, stone or brick, elsewhere.

Remember also the ruins, often majestic,
sometimes humble.

While you walk retrace parts of history, visible to
memory.

Even the meticulous cross-section of this rock
where mica was deposited in the shape of a
temple.

Over there, it looks like a miniature Luxor.

Right here, at one's feet, it's Chartres.

Yesterday, a piece of the Acropolis brought back in a bag.

And today, unbelievably, it's Angkor Wat, finely delineated.

Now the world's treasures fallen, inexplicably, in this savage land (barely mentioned in scholarly books).

Now the return of diverse life-forms, museum erected only by chance.

Sometimes, faced with so many marvels, one decides to stay home a while.

At home, inside or out in the yard, if it's nice.

In the evenings, the stars take over.

Sometimes, one chooses retreat, deprivation.

Numerous stone irises peering from the vault, watch you, eclipsing other images.

Better leave them alone.

They're preparing the next rough path.

Certain ones leave the celestial retina. They run off, heads under water, blind for millennia, luminous streaks.

Opera's final scene, they disappear. Adieu space and time, adieu eternity, they say one last time.

Or then, one doesn't recall anything. Outrageous forgetfulness.

At the window, something motions singing and crying, flying and turning from the yard to the sea.

Few flowers grow in this spot, few stems stand up
to the salt and wind.

One invents gardens of stones, discovers Nordic
cactuses, within.

Through peregrinations and returns, one invents
destinies.

In the thin claw marks, last testaments.

Dreaming of Provençal gardens, of West Indian flora, one wonders what strange artisan, angel or devil and why? made you run aground there.

Covertly, your rebellious ground reclaims its rights, restores its stunning magnificence.

Thus silent, you put your heart back in the work of surviving, again you turn over the hourglass.

A fistful of moist sand settles quietly; the world is in hand.

Identical, the sphinx, eyelids closed or faces mutilated like Iroquois chiefs, impressed on the stele, debris of bows, splints, kings' tombs.

Beforehand, everything's possible, all the tumult. And not long ago, so many accidents.

Like today without anyone thinking too much about it.

The hand sculpting caresses, the hand lets slip however.

Broken up, everything returns to limbo, to formlessness.

Until a new object, until the next impulse.

Waiting, sand around the land's waters and in its very body, deep in the desert.

We don't know any more, we don't know quite what collapsed, then reassembled.

We wander about on the look out for explanations.

Does beauty hold a grudge?

Retracing our steps, we won't think about it any more. Until tomorrow.

Until that tantalizing morning of idleness.

Once night has fallen, the masters of signs are no longer visible.

Boring into dream, nailing down the distant interior, the lost steps.

Light strokes, but persistent, the quest makes do with little.

What unknown watchwoman, migrant friend, will have copied the prints exactly? And when?

They thought they'd seized tangible evidence, here, however, is what's left, immeasurable, abundant debris.

Obscurity, haven of the humble.

The world's childbirths announced by a cry, are, for the time being, faint murmurings.

The midwife's image flees the mirage, has no pond to bend over.

She's mourning lost paradise: people, things, time.

With each successive photo, wrest time's insane course, transform its nostalgia into proof.

Trials of the frozen moment, of the stable frame: create the future with the past.

But one knows only too well that the present, unless one takes oneself for god, is always old hat.

Thus remains, muse on the run.

First take, reprint, beginning already repeated.

Born abstraction? concretion of origin? calculation? tophus? One gives up on all counts, even in celestial matters, if there are any, the cat has our tongue.

It's like that, one can't do anything about it.

Certain people purr: so, why bother? why this dream?

No response, one slips to the side.

Frivolous tourists, clear out! The esplanade is bored with you.

Compared with uncertain paths, it has the gift of a modest miracle.

Seeds and dust on one's soles and in one's hair, wind, sunbeams.

Now shouldered, the momentum is sustained.

Here, the archaic muses savour the crumbs. It's their feast.

When desire breaks through to embrace the details on a grand scale, the walk becomes a march, alert demeanour, robust decision, vigour that propels it forward.

At the opposite end, wandering that wells up from the depths of the body, that comes from foreign lands, intimate fragments that one has lugged around since the time of migrant ancestors.

March and wandering, upstream and downstream throbbing and untangling.

Then buckling down again until the next departure.

Dream the spirit of places never visited, make of them one's future books.

At each turn, unrecognized Saharas unroll their alphabets in the beige folds.

Then an isolated firedamp explosion obliterates landmarks, the homeland wastes away in the distance.

The earth too has its patience.

On this harsh blue morning, one comes back to this other mother, clay that, under its slow metamorphic pressure, gave us slate.

Only in the darkroom, will illegible letters appear on it.

For the unfinished reading, perpetually re-begun. In the inner realm.

Photographed under the microscope, stone thinks, its age stirs.

Along the gold-bearing veins, the heart beats, an enclosed heart.

Right there.

All the subtle precision of the world in the manipulation of the tanning knife. Don't lose the thread, it's the only mission.

Footsteps set off again on the immense beige expanse unfolding to infinity.

In the exile of dream's image, even though god is invisible, the sound's absence stands guard, silenced verb.

Tunics flying in the wind, sailboats glide towards the breast of dunes, milky, rustling silk, down there.

Very far away. Even to the promised land.

So long ago.

Other birthings, under other metamorphic outcroppings, yield garnet and granite.

Captured at dawn, I addressed them with this supplication:

Mimics, now look at me. Look at me, I'm speaking in my sleep. Write me until dawn.

See, under your vitreous gangue.

Tender are the opaque nights that leave the brilliance of stars unchecked.

Under the cupola other geographies light up.

Someone left the troglodytes' gear in the cloakroom. On the moon's horn, suspended enigmas.

In reality, a blaze that calls and stays. Wordless.

One cannot of course represent it, the dream follows itself.

Secrets are nailed shut, speech of flesh, souls, waters.

They prevail, day as well as night, elsewhere or here.

This is not a mirage. A glass will soon be raised to this unique evidence.

Things put down there set us back to zero again.

For the thinking being, this puddle is only mud.

But the sand itself remembers silt.

A passing thought on the undatable code that flint left everywhere.

Without the icebox sea that precedes it, I would not be busy contemplating this green copper silicate in my hand.

Objects marry us.

In the nuptial chamber, our children were born from chrysocolla and nuclear rocks.

So many paper weddings for these mineral mouths, foreseen pacts, banquets.

IV

READING THE STONES

In odd moments
we film the clouds

Or the birds

Time gained
that humbly sets its tokens
ablaze

Or perhaps
the plants

Read the sky
or the stones

Take the wind
the water
the salt
the sand
as one takes time

As one takes one's time

Upset
by the tiniest wrinkle

Understanding it
in every line

Baring to its clutches
the naked
word

Losing one's time this way

Write the stones
as they present themselves

I know illiterate people
who are versed in them

I know inscriptions
that are languages
which language overlooks

Outside the poem's language
in a state of shock

Outside the law

Write the stones
as people have read them

With this peculiar language
escaped from school

Offered to the sky's board

To the desks of migratory birds

Passing by

The chalk came from eons ago
the slate equally old

And the windows
through which one goes out
into the fields

Constructed
to keep
indoors

Read the signs
that chance alone
has cherished

The hand
from time to time sweeps aside
or the breath dusts

Write what the eye perceives
close up

Write beyond the buried
the interred

Trust an old
acquaintance
who comes
from someplace or other

Whom one does not understand
entirely

Her understanding falters
in a distance
resembling

The blind holes
of the earth's body
of its skin

There are sometimes
petroglyphs
written
by a man

Or a woman

Doubtless also
by children
intent in reproducing
their parents'
pictograms

Or simply
in inventing them

In these tongues
thoughts
translated into images

Of accustomed objects
tools
weapons

Human bodies

When thoughts
become grandiose

They are suns
moons
dressing
women
men
children

All the visible
constellations
covering over
the mysteries
of destiny

Often people etch
the animals

Who fly
crawl
or walk

They are taken
as witnesses

Of the dramas
of the sky
of the land
of the waters

A library
of animals

Excavate
to grasp
(even partially)

Time's
gears
in human
space

Celebrate this resurrection

These stories
in snatches

Taken from the rock
tomb

Brought back
as if reduced to shadows
ash

The world's fiancés
quietly
greeted

In another mode
the song
when no name
is recorded

Yes, inorganic
matter
thinks too

The entire poem in the mind
of the unknown poet

Recalling
stone to stone

The stone of darkness

Along with the vivid memory
of the living
departed

Stele on stele
double impression

One brings these strata
together

The mute waves
suddenly confiding in

Those at hand
already speaking

Most often
they're quiet
among themselves

As if
the apparent excessiveness
of places
of time

Invalidated
the night's bar
under which
our incessant words

Fall
nonstop

Read the stones
as they were
written

Either alone
unaligned
by themselves

Or
through all these ascendants

That over them
crisscross tutelary
plans

Wills

Read each chapter
right away

Enter into the searing light
(it's a bequest
to take all)

Then study the details

The mineral syntax
the grammar
the lexicon
the alphabet

Through the voiceless
masses
see the solitudes
married

These souls
without mouths

These spirits
without voice

Greet very softly
the memory
of the verb

Of erased time

The eternal return
extinguished

Defy
the heraldic sleep
under the moist
mosses

Follow
the cursive birdlime

A trickle
of saliva
in place
of a fixed
mouth

Life
takes odd
detours

Sinuous
paths
not yet source

Imitating
the design
of the snake

Who came shortly
after
the birth
of water

Anonymous
and enduring
autographs

Distributed
wherever the
liquid
roads take them

Or gusts
of wind

Just
allusive signatures

Dorsal drawing
of the humble
fowl

Whose name one
hunts

Tenuousness of the message

A single vein
underwater
reveals

The departed
epoch

The immensity
of a world map
under the quartz
needles

Flux of species

On the bistre-coloured limestone
the goldsmith got the better
of our cold gloom

The slow worm's eye
touches
this human
half-heart

Venture even farther
where that wasn't thought of

Braid
the lost soul
with the first
desires

Go off
towards the intimate
country

Strange long hair
to untangle

Against all odds
a crossing
between sky
and abyss

When it went well
undefined

Challenge
of the undertaking
on the shadows'
crest

Crystal flash
like
a cry

Translate
as closely as possible
the sheer
distance

Delicacy
of the lines
that one folds
and unfolds

On leaves
bathed
in watchful
memory

Mistakenly believed
asleep

Grasp
in the approximate
casting

Well above
the glacial breeze
a few glimmers

Voices offered
stitched by immemorial
hands

That seem to move
outstretched

Frozen in their
movements

On the look-out
for bad weather
for predators

For some gigantic
cataclysm

One imagines
the souls
at the moment
of passage

Going off towards the unknown
their mouths agape

Beyond
catastrophes
love inferred

From so many signs
so many forms

Is only
its record

One leaves
for a while
what led us
there

The image was a patient
guide

Sounding the hour
when the debris
(of space, of time)
is no longer measured
in hardened form

Nothing
from here or there
can grapple

With these inalienable
beings
things

Time and space
wed
on the eternal
bed

Intertwined
concave
shadowy spheres and
lines
revealed

A few lights
on the reliefs

Smiles cut
into the flint

Final tears
of clay

There would be the music
of the ode

Perhaps an opera

Some baroque libretto

A transversal beauty
with the laughter of rhymes
that lightly brush against
unchanging human sorrows
washed of all tears

That seem to quake
as they go by

In the dawn
and night
of time

Their chords
would unfold

Violins and harps
on the horizon
anthracite

All ears
sated

All movements
epochs
replete

Under the great earthy
canopy
where mists
float out

Buried crosses
furrow the expanse

Totems
proof

The orchestra
plays backwards

Hearing sensitive
to its touch

A lapse comes
when music alone

Hears
what defies
understanding

Universal language

Invented
people say
by some blind
divinity

One day
in the fan-shaped
crystals

Green
emerald

I saw
Lot's wife
her head turned
too soon

It was in Aveyron

I greeted her
(does one ever know)

Another time
in the Yukon
(this is a story)

A finger of siderite
stuck
onto the crystal

Seen
at the bottom
of the deposit

Under the curve
of the breast
the entire body
of a child

I rejoiced

It was night
at day
when darkness
lurked

Noon, midnight
one never
knew

It had been night
at day
for so long
now

I had returned
to obscurity
my solo
uncertain

In the mica-laced
sheet
miniatures
drifted

Under the milky
ice field
this audible
creaking

Between temple
and shoulder
sketched

Just by listening

Sonorous
words

Then the return
of ice
to the mosses

Of tundra
to the bushes
to the fruit trees

Still the long
walk
across
dense woods

Soon villages
cities

Music
of people
rediscovered

At the four cardinal
points
compressed
onto a single stave

The recollection
of centuries
stubbornly surviving

Just for you

The recollection
and the lapses of memory

Major modes
and minor
just for you

Passing by

Fables
at first
hillocky

Give up
one
after
the other

Bored
with the granular
stelae

G, F, C

Each in its key

One day
I'll go off
towards the jewelled
countryside

To touch ruby-rich
sapphire-bright
fields

Far off
in Burma
in Kashmir
in the Ariège

I'll listen to
Das Lied von der Erde

Arborescent

This music
from which words are excavated
vibrates
so intensely

That very little of it
would make limbs
liberated from stalactites
fly

And the heart
slip off
fording
towards
infinity

Bible
Torah
or some apocryphal
letter

A book open
to the limits

That treelike
spits
torrents of tears
and bursts of laughter

That snows
frail spheres
in the Prussian
blue
dawn

In the aria
that would be time's
offering

May the iron of my blood
dissolve
into the unrefined
ore

When the crystal
filigree
blends in

By some liquid
magic
now
my very eyes
riveted on
the eternal

Write
with death's thread
that will stitch every mouth
bind every hand

Write
the elusive
golden morning
under the rosy
sands

Thread words
in the shade

No matter where
the path

Thread
in the light
(this unique
evidence)

With a minuscule
needle's eye
where the birthing
sage

Pulls out life
wherever it falls

When life's
fabric
tears

I am of this rocky
planet's
mantel

This lunar
spasm
that saw me
born

I am of this uterine
abyss
from which rustles
the bush

I'm going off somewhere
from whence
(so they whisper to me)
they came

As long as there is
a breath
there will be writing

Overflowing
link after link
back to the beginning
the song

I'll pass away
before this imagined
timeless
finale

Amber slipping
from pass to pass
on top
of the world

Rimouski 1994-Montréal 1998

NOTES

The title of this book comes from the first line of Charles Baudelaire's sonnet, "La Beauté."

Kindred spirits: *L'Ecriture des pierres*, Roger Caillois; *Pensées sous les nuages*, Philippe Jaccottet; *Ce qui est*, Christian Hubin.

A few poems from this collection have appeared in *Metamorphoses, Beacons, Saranac Review, Confrontation, Great River Review, Gulf Coast, The Marlboro Review, International Poetry Review, and Mid-American Review.*

Born in Amqui, Québec, Madeleine Gagnon has published over forty books of poetry and prose in Québec and France. Although Gagnon's work is firmly rooted in North American mythology, history, and culture, she has published significant works dealing with the situation of women in war-torn countries and the impact of prolonged suffering on people's minds and spirits. Her novel, *Je m'appelle Bosnia,* published by VLB éditeur in 2005, is a haunting, frank look at a young woman's struggle to survive without sacrificing her identity or her aspirations. Member of the Académie des lettres du Québec since 1987, Gagnon is the recipient of numerous distinguished literary awards, including the Governor General of Canada's Award in 1991 for *Chant pour un Québec lointain,* the Prix Arthur-Buies for her lifetime body of work, and the Prix Athanase-David du Québec in 2002. In 2007, l'Hexagone brought out *À l'ombre des mots/poèmes 1964-2006* in their prestigious collection Rétrospectives. Her books have been translated into Spanish and English.

For Madeleine Gagnon, the interrelationship between the planet's cultures far surpasses the conflicts and differences between nations and peoples. Geology, music, painting, sculpture, poetry, the wonderful art of daydreaming or loafing on a beach all add up to something unexpected and compelling that allows us to celebrate the beauty and harmony that underlie our ephemeral existence. *Stone Dream* takes the reader on a voyage through time and cultures. We marvel at past wonders, great architecture, fabulous jewels, strange and exotic music; we emerge in the twentieth and twenty-first centuries to contemplate the fate of those at war, to join their sorrow, and praise their courage. We learn something about ourselves as we read these poems and something about poetry itself. Gagnon takes us on the ultimate trip a poet can offer; the vast journey through our collective unconscious to produce the living poem, the dream of stone that so tantalized and provoked Baudelaire.

Andrea Moorhead is editor of *Osiris* and author of several books of poetry in French and in English.